ELEMENTS OF THE SOUL

INHALE

POEMS   N E

CW01084326

EMILY ALBOU

To my chosen family

Coming Soon to a Heart Near You

More from this author:

Elements of the soul: Exhale (Poems Volume Two)

Contents

Small Talk	7
Advocate	8
Amour à moi	9
Anouchka	10
Anxiety	11
Arrogance	12
Avatar	13
Breaking up	14
Bumble Boy	15
Bumble Boy - when we met	16
Catharsis	17
Chapter 1	18
Come Back	20
Contact List	21
Courage	22
Cretinous	23
Cutie	24
Devotion	25
Disappointment	26
Disbelief	27
Do you see me?	28
Dracula	29
Dreams	30
Dusk	31
Emotion	32
Exhale	33
Fate	34
Feel	35
Fool for you	36
Goodbye	37
Healing	38
Healing – 2	39
Healing – 3	40
Heartbreak	42
Here I am	43
History	44
I am all of the men I have loved	45
I am so tired	46
I like my face	47
I wonder	48
Inadequacy	49
Incognito	50

Indignant	51
Inevitable	52
Interlude	53
Interlude 2	54
Interlude 2.1	55
Interlude 3	56
Interlude 4	57
Interlude 5	58
Interlude 6	59
Interlude 7	60
Interlude 8	61
Interlude 9	62
Interlude 10	63
Interlude 11	64
Introspection	65
Iris	66
June 2018	67
Kintsugi	68
Lion	69
Lies	70
Layers	71
Life talks	72
Life talks 2.0	73
Living	74
Lost & Found	75
Love Me Hate Me	76
Love who you will	77
Milano	78
Mount Olympus	79
My Broken Pieces	80
My Heart is a Palace	81
New Life	83
NWTKE	84
Ode to Egypt	86
Ode to My Body	87
Ode to Pants	88
'On This Day'	89
Oslo	90
Pedestal	91
Perspective	92
Powerless	93
Priorities	94
Promise me no promises	95
Puppets	96

Purpose	97
Regret (short-lived)	98
Repeat views	99
Rhythm	100
SILENCIO	101
Self-care	102
Self-loathing	103
Selfishness	105
The Bay	106
The Bay 2	107
Sisters	108
Soft Tissue Injury	109
Solinne	110
Special Needs	111
Stephanie's Table	112
Subconscious	113
Summer	114
Summer nights	115
Summer nights – 2	116
Summer nights – 3	117
Summer nights – 4	118
Tattoo	119
Tattoo 2	120
The Mask	121
The Elephant in the room	122
The Maybe-One	124
The Problem with Betrayal	126
Therapy	127
Tomb Raider	128
v2	129
Views	130
Visceral	131
What if...	132
Wildfire	133
Wishful Thinking	134
20:20 vision	135
14:58	136
Thank You	137
Epilogue	138
About the author	140

Small Talk

I was asked today what I do.
I write poetry, I said.
What kind? Sonnets, prose?

No. The kind I pour my heart and soul into.
The kind that isn't defined by the structure of its lines.
The kind that carries my voice.

Advocate

Sucking the joy from my soul
Sucking the youth from my skin
Sucking the life out of me,
My spirit
Evaporating
Slowly wisping from my fingertips.
Every word that I write
Every case that I argue
If I win, if I lose
The cost is more than you pay me
Yet the price will never be enough.
Every time I have to choose
Until I forget
The extent to which
I am drained.
The extent to which
I am forgotten.
In constant conflict
The Romantic v. The Realist
One can't exist without the other
And yet one
Whilst sustaining me
Is slowly
But surely
Killing me.

Amour à moi

Amour
Amour à moi
Dis-moi pourquoi
Tu me plais tant.

Ton sourire m'inspire,
Ta voix, ton rire
Même tes soupirs
Je veux tout de toi.

Te connaître, admettre
Que ce que tu m'apportes
Je ne le trouve qu'en toi.
Tu es un roi.

Roi de mes rêves,
De mon imagination
De mes orgasmes.

Journées au rythme rapide
Au rythme lent
Journées qui passent...

Ta curiosité m'éveille
Tes baisers m'évoquent
Tes tendresses m'adoucissent.

Tel le goût de la réglisse
Je te croque tu me mords
Je t'adore.

Anouchka

I am so
Fucking
Terrified
Of the day
You will leave me.
Not that you will leave
By choice.
The Gods of life
Or death
Or misfortune
Will take you and keep you for themselves.
How could they not?
You are a living angel.
You are beauty
You are strength
You are love.
You are the light
Of my life
And I pray
That somehow
Someday
You will know
How much
I love you.
That when they
Come for you
You will not be scared
For you will know
That your light
Cannot be
Starved
Cannot be
Stolen.
You shine stronger
And brighter
Than all the constellations
In the sky
And when the time
Comes
For the curtain to fall
My light will dim
But will not leave
For Your light
Lives on,
Within.

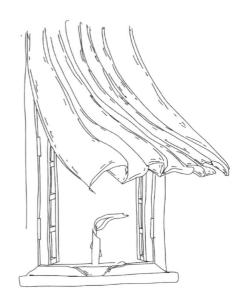

Anxiety

As the light glares down upon me,
Sweat trickles down my face.
When will they ignore me?
How will I save face?

I don't have much to tell, you see
I haven't lived that long.
I spent my life by a wishing well
A life spent in song.

The audience goes quiet
The claps seem to fade.
Eyes look up expectant
Can't you see? It's a charade.

Arrogance

It is an arrogance
Of our generation
That we think
We are better off alone.

The time isn't right
You don't yet own a home
Your job isn't stable
You've just taken out a loan.

You're scared of obligations
Of being trapped or tied down.
But love doesn't trap you
It's the other way around.

Herein lies the secret:
The time is never right.
The secret, pray, do listen
Is to find love and hold on tight.

Avatar

You are more worthy

Of all my poetry

Than anyone else

I know.

And yet for you, I cannot write.

The wound is still too deep,

5 years do not heal overnight.

Breaking up

I cried
You hugged me.
It wasn't enough.

I cried
You left me.
I wasn't enough.

Bumble Boy

You set my soul on fire.

Bumble Boy - when we met

I thought if I went home with you
I wouldn't see you again.
The next morning when I woke up
It wasn't even 10.
I snuck out of your apartment
I had somewhere to be
And yet you called and asked me out
Almost immediately.
Then we went on our first date
(We did things in reverse)
Over coffee, talk of philosophy,
I realised I was cursed.
For looking at your smile then,
And looking at it now,
Has the effect of stopping my breath
In a life-changing pow-wow.
"You're actually quite smart" you said, "educated and well read"
"Well what else did you think I would be? An air-head blonde only here to please?"
That was when you grabbed my hand
And looked me in the eyes
And whispered you didn't want this to end
- to my great surprise.
And so we went to dinner, Italian was on the cards
And as you sat across me, you couldn't help but stare.
I thought it might be my charm, until you did declare:
"I've never seen someone made so happy simply by eating food"
"Well, I'm quite a catch, it's really all it takes to improve my mood!"
We walked back to your flat again
This time hand in hand
Oblivious to others there
We really didn't care.
Then I met your flatmate
(I was sober this time round)
He seemed confused albeit amused
That I had returned.
So that is how we started
- or what of it I recall.
But it isn't how we ended,
Sadly not at all.

Catharsis

Scooping out the rotten emotion
Each ball
Perfectly round
Plopped into a cone.

An ice-cream
I'll never eat.
I'll stare at it in the display
Behind the lights and plastic sheet

A chocolate-filled center
Hazelnuts round the side.
Goodbye, rotten emotion
You are no longer mine.

Chapter 1

We met and we fell in love.
That part was easy.
Smooth sailing.
Most days, at least.

Love carried us for 2.5 years.
Then Love tripped and fell.
Her bag on the floor,
Contents strewn everywhere.

Our relationship abandoned
To the cigarette butts
And takeaway wrappers
Lining the streets and the gutters.

That was the first time
You broke my heart.

I thought I would never recover.

Then you came back,
My knight in shining armour.
Healed me
Held me
Loved me
Cherished me.
I thought you would marry me.

You broke my heart
A second time.
This time you didn't look back.

Seconds are appetising,
Third helpings non-existent.
I was relinquished to
An after-thought.
An item in your life
That no longer had effect.
Not worthy, even,
Of communication;
Silence was all
You would give to me.

I stopped waiting for you.
Eventually.
It took me 18 months.

People think we do not speak,
But you still visit me in my sleep.

Come Back

When I say
Wish, pray
Plead
"Come back!"
As I'm begging
On my knees
It is not you
I'm crying for.

It is my happiness
My heart
My joy
My youth
My ability to love blindly
And to give myself
Whole,
Unsuspectingly.

Not to the next person
Who may come along
But to myself.
I need me.
My heart needs me.
I need to
Come back.
To me.

Contact List

The contact list
Of letdown.
That is what
This has become.

Another day
Another disappointment.
Damaging friends
Breeding resentment.

I open up my phone
To see who I can call,
Who could support me
Through it all?

And there I am faced
With the reality.
It's no wonder
I'm questioning my sanity.

Name after name
Of people I did trust
But who made it clear
It wasn't love, it was lust.

Courage

When did I get the courage
To try with someone like you
Someone I hadn't met before
Someone I barely knew.
Did I see it written
Somewhere in the stars
That if I let you kiss me
Our love might live and last.

Cretinous

Cretins how I hate you so
You fill my life with waste and woe
Always there to bring me down
You'd think you're trying to take my crown.

But cretins, hark, woe is not me
I live a life of fantasy
Until I rise I will not fall
You can't take me, I take them all.

Cutie

"Cutie. You're a good mix. Cheese and Potatoes: the best of both worlds"
You said,
As I lay there in bed
Sated and doe eyed.
Little did I know you were feeding me lies.
Why am I even surprised?
I barely knew you.
The problem is you knew me
And you played me, used me, screwed me,
Until you devoured me -
Whole -
In a fit of ecstasy.
Until I was nothing but air between your lips:
A forgotten fantasy.

Devotion

I fear the scar on my heart will never heal.

Your face imprinted in my eyes
Your smell
Your taste
Your smile
Your laughter
Your stubble
Your hands,
No longer there to hold me.

Is this what devotion looks like?
Loving someone who no longer wants to be loved?

Disappointment

The most disappointing thing
About you
Is that you turned out to be
Unremarkable.

Disbelief

I thought you knew what you wanted

I thought you wanted me.

Tell me, how could I be so blind

How is it I could not see?

That all you ever wanted

Was nowhere to be found;

A dream, a myth, a fairytale

Anti-climactic, moribund.

Do you see me?

I am not here for your pleasure.

Dracula

I went and named him
Dracula.
Not a blood-sucker
Actually quite sweet
But with teeth. Teeth.
Teeth teeth teeth teeth teeth!
Somehow his teeth were kissing me.

Dreams

I tell everyone I'm over you
That I don't think of you anymore.
Why is it then I dream of you
More than I did before.

In my dreams we're happy,
Smiling, and in love,
You pull me in for the sweetest kiss
And time seems to stop.

When daylight comes to wake me
My dreams no longer there
The sadness still inside me
And longing for repair.

Dusk

Dusk is setting
Light has come to pass
The water is still.
Silent reflections
Things unsaid
Unspoken
Unmoved
Always felt.
The light's reflection
Playing off the lake
My
Mirror.
I can see it
And myself
So clearly.
A scene of
Serenity
I have not felt
In so long.
I feel like I am
Home.
The light comes to pass
The moon reflecting
Her glow
Her glory
Her peace.
Tonight the night
Is where I belong.
I'm ready to say my piece.

Emotion

I feel the emotion
Bubble up inside me,
Like a popcorn kernel
Ready to burst.
Except a popcorn kernel
Is so small.
And my emotion
Is so BIG.

Exhale

I stop breathing

When I think of you.

As if scared

That in exhaling

I might breathe out

All that is still left of

You within me.

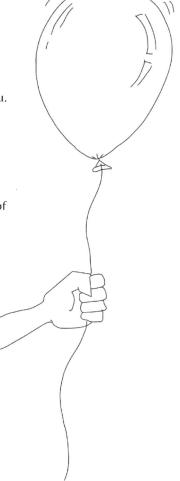

Fate

Maybe I'm crazy
Maybe I'm bold
Maybe I wish my
Fortune was told
To those who seek
Affection the most.

- You see

My heart is more than
An elegant host.
It is made,
I believe,
To love with its All
To comfort, to cherish, to have
and behold.
And maybe I'm crazy,
But I'm honest, sincere
And right now all I want
Is for you to be here
To have and to hold
To melt in your arms
As your lover, best friend,
Although truth be told,

- The fire alarm goes off. Disturbs
my thoughts, my flow, but not my
feelings.

My feelings remain
I'm still the same
And this is my point:
I FEEL.
I feel so deeply it aches
I feel SO deeply that I am
prepared
To swallow my pride
And to call you back. Again.

Feel

Don't be afraid to feel.
It's how you know you're alive.

Fool for you

I see you in places
You do not even exist,
Within strangers' faces,
Couples sharing a kiss.

I see you in places
You do not even belong,
And pray to God's graces
That what I saw there was wrong.

At the heart of my soul,
In my deepest desires,
Amidst the gut-wrenching sadness,
You will find there a fire.

A fire of hope,
A fire of love,
A fire which burns
As bright as a dove

And as it spreads through my body
Flames licking my skin
Thoughts of you consume me:
My ultimate sin.

Maybe one day I'll forget you,
Maybe one day I'll move on,
But that day is not this one
For the fire still burns strong.

Goodbye

As I turn and say goodbye
Remember I did not leave.

As I turn and see you cry
Remember this please.

That my heart cannot love, give, nurture
To those who only take.

Some may call it strength,
I call it fate.

As I turn and walk away
1000 questions still on my lips

Watch my outline fade away
My final kiss still on your lips.

As I fade out of your sight
Please don't feel ashamed.

You may have lost. You may have failed.
But to you it was just a game.

Healing

It was never consensual.

So how could the healing be consensual?

There was nothing for him to heal.

I had to heal myself.

Healing – 2

I am going to fall in love with you.
That I already know.
It is inevitable.

Like rapids rushing
Towards a waterfall.

Now is the sweetest moment.
I know it is coming
But I am not yet victim
To the fever.
To the chills.

Now is the moment of sweetness.
Of balmy summer nights
Of staring at the stars
And hoping you'll be the sun.

Of hoping you're the one.

Healing – 3

Your hand grazes my knee
Tentatively;
A shot of electricity
Bolts through my body
I sit there
For just a second.

As I feel my heart
Pounding
In my chest.

Excitement mixed with anxiety.

I read you my poetry
Not just my poetry
But your poem.
Not just your poem
But what it did to me.

I see shock
Hurt
Pain
Worry
Empathy
Protectiveness

A mix of emotion
So strong
I don't know if you will be able
To contain it.

I say it's OK. We don't have to talk
about it
I wasn't planning on it anyway;
You insist we do.
Clearly I am hurting.
You want to make it right.

We thrash it out
Less of a tennis match
More of a tag race
Your feelings, my feelings
Your hurt, my hurt
Your truth
My truth
Different but both valid.

Pause.
The words released
Hanging in the air
Like a samurai's sword
Waiting to find its target.

But its target is not here anymore.

The sword now a dazzling gold
With a ruby in its helm
Its blade blindingly bright.

As you pick me up, kiss me
My mouth searching for yours
With a hunger,
With a passion
I did not even know I had within me.

With every kiss,
Every lick,
Every groan,
My body becoming once more
My own.

Heartbreak

Sometimes
I wish
I could
Hate you.

When I hate you
I don't miss you.
When I hate you
It doesn't hurt.

You cut my limbs off
One by one,
Slowly peeled out my heart.
An excruciating piece of art.

Back inside you put
A stone.
A ruby.
Red. Cold. Unmoving.

I feel numb
When I think of anyone.
Then I think of you
And I still can't hate you.

I miss you
So. Much.
So much that it hurts
To breathe.

Every inhale, exhale
Stabbing my throat
Piercing my lungs
Why live if it's without you?

Then I see you,
The ruby inside of me
Twitches.
Wanting to beat.

Until you look away,
Walk away
Again
And again
And again.

Here I am

I am your wildest dreams
That you never fulfilled.
I am everything you dreamed of
But were too scared to try.

A life rich in fantasy
Love as my only guide
Full of vibrant colours
And nothing to hide.

Fear does not live here
Adventure is where I belong.
Courage is my companion
And Fate is my song.

So go ahead, hate me.
Criticise me, condemn me.
As frivolous, exuberant
"You're always travelling, do you never work!"

My happiness provoking such bitterness
Masked behind a smile
Betrayed by your impatience
And eyes in denial.

I am what you could have been.
But tough luck.
I am not you.
I am me.

History

If there is
One person
I am not afraid of
Being imperfect with
It is you.

You have seen
Everything
There is to see.

You have seen me look better
Look worse
You have seen me laugh,
You have seen me cry
You have held me
Comforted me
Laughed with me
Laughed at me.

You have loved me
You have hated me
I have hurt you
You have hurt me.

We have left each other
Found our way back to one another
Lost each other, again.

If there is
One person
I have nothing
To hide from
It is you.

You have seen
Everything
Already.

I am all of the men I have loved

I am all of the men I have loved.
I am strong, I am suave
I see myself in their smiles
My smile, embedded in their hearts.
My outline, embedded in their eyes.

Of course you are dating after me,
How else will you forget me?
I am unforgettable.
I have left an indelible mark.
Not quite a scar - scars fade.

And every time you meet someone,
She might look like me,
Ever so slightly
But she won't have my energy.
Elle ne sera pas Emily.

I know you won't forget me
But I truly do wish you well
And that your memory

Of my kiss
On your lips
My whisper
In your ear
My smile, next to you
As I wake up

May give you some comfort
In knowing that you lost me
Mistakenly.

I am so tired

I am so tired
Tired of loving the men who weren't right
I am so tired
I no longer want to try
I am so tired
I just want to dance as the sun sets
Music filling my heart and my soul
I am so tired
I no longer want to think
Pass me a drink and a beat
I am so tired
That the next person will have to sweep
Me off my feet
And carry me home.

I like my face

When you tell me
To change my face
Remove my moles
Laser them off
It is not a criticism of me.
It is your own self-loathing,
Consuming you entirely,
That I see.
Can you not see my beauty
My glory
My strength
My light
Radiating out of me
Like a long lost lover.
I found it again
And now it is here to stay
You cannot take that away
Not with your words
Or your fists
Light lasts an eternity.

I wonder

I wonder if
You get on the train
And look around
As I do.

I wonder if
You wonder if
I'm sat there
Looking for you.

I wonder if
You saw me
The same way
I saw you.

I wonder if
You hope to see me sitting there
Legs crossed, smile wide
Sitting in your favourite underwear.

I wonder if
You see my outline
The way I see yours
Everywhere around me.

I wonder if
You hope you'll see me
Again, get to greet me
And maybe love me.

I wonder if
You miss me too
The same way
That I am missing you
I wonder. I wonder if.

Inadequacy

What would it take for you to love me?
What would I have to do?
Would I have to sit and smile
Or chase after you.

What would it take for you to see me?
Where would I have to go?
Should I climb the nearest mountain
Or star in a show.

What would it take for you to hear me?
What would I have to sing?
Would you want me loud and fierce
Or quietly whispering.

What would it take for you to want me?
What would I have to write?
A song, a gift, an anthem
Or a lullaby at night.

Incognito

The pauper is in

The Palace

Throwing

Wild parties

Of debauchery

Of destruction.

Indignant

I was indignant from the way you treated me,
As nothing but a taster on a buffet platter.
You failed to see the exquisite delicacy
That I am.
You failed as a man.

Inevitable

We reached the end
Before we even began.

Interlude

I went walking
Into a desert of blue
I wasn't looking
And yet I found you
An oasis of green
In a land so dry
Promise me one thing
Just don't make me cry
We climbed the mountains
We leapt to the sea
An adventure called life
Or so you told me

Interlude 2

The pain in my heart

Cries out

Like a howling wolf

Under a full moon.

Interlude 2.1

And I spend my time wishing my days away in daydreams of faraway places with mysterious faces wishing that's where I could be.

Interlude 3

Dénudée. Dénouée. Exquise.

Interlude 4

"It's OK, I'll see you tomorrow;
It's not like my dick's going to fall off
Overnight."
                    - *before I never saw you again*

Interlude 5

I am the one you won't forget.

I am the one you will regret.

Interlude 6

I would have loved you.

If you'd let me.

Interlude 7

I was hoping you would call.

Did I matter at all?

Interlude 8

"Do you wear your lipstick

Just so I can kiss it off?"

Interlude 9

"Is every day with you like this?"

Interlude 10

I dreamt of you again last night.

I wish it wasn't so.

Interlude 11

I am so lucky

To have

Loved

So many.

Introspection

You made me feel worthless.
After making me whole.
You took my heart
And placed it high:
No one could deny
Our Love.
Until you dropped it.
Smashed it.
Scarred it.
Breaking my heart and my confidence with it.
Why don't you want me? After all, you're the one who broke me.

Iris

I will have a daughter
And I will name her Iris.

Iris.
Not the apple of my eye
But Iris:
She who can see.

She will be fierce.
She will be whole.

June 2018

You spent your summer solstice
Reading my blog.
The never-ending day.
The light you can't put out.

Kintsugi

I read somewhere that when something is broken the Japanese put it
back together and fill the cracks with gold.
I like to think of my heart like that: broken, but beautiful. Decorated
with gold lines.

One is deep and wide, running right through the middle: the love
that changed me; the gold that saved me.

My fear is what if my heart breaks so many times, with so many gold
lines, that it becomes a heart of gold. Frozen, solid, incapable of love.
A Midas heart.

My heart is made for living. Loving. Beating. Not breaking.

Lion

What's your favourite animal?
A lion!
Why?
It's strong, courageous, loyal, fearless
How I think of myself.
You said it's what I'm looking for
In a partner.
True.

But I am also a lion.
I roar under the sun
I protect those I love
A wild mane
Glistening
Ready to challenge everything
Can you see me?
Powerful.

Why then since I've met you
Do I not feel
Like a lion
Anymore?
My insides are in turmoil.
No longer serene
Or calm
Or, even, fierce.

Questioning, anxious
Like a long loop
Of twisted paper
Waiting for release.
I don't even know what I'm looking for
What I need to make it right
And that also is so unlike me,
Where is my insight?

The lion is still inside me
But I think it's hiding
Within.

Because since I met you
I don't want to fight
Anymore
I want to let you
Win.

Lies

I am emotionally raw.

Every inch of my body,
every crease, every fold

Pulled back, peeled off

Exposed.

Exposed to his insanity,

To his necrotising words

To his lies.

Lies

Which cover my body

In patterns and designs,

Lies

Which slide across me

So smoothly

Covering me in ink.

At first, beautiful

But slowly covering every
inch of my face

Until I can't see, hear, can't
breathe.

Covering every inch of me

Until I no longer recognise
myself.

Who am I?

What have you made of
me?

Layers

Can you see the softness in my steel?

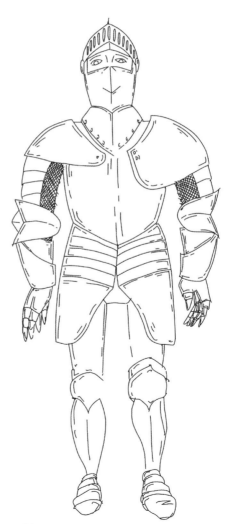

Life talks

"Does any human have all the answers?"

- No. Because the questions always change.

Life talks 2.0

It's crazy how we want what's bad for us.
Like doughnuts.
And shitty men.

Living

Leave the past behind

Let it go completely

You are not a tape

You cannot live in rewind.

Lost & Found

In the Lost & Found
Is where I found your face
A life spent together
Of which there is no trace.

Amongst the umbrellas and the gloves
Lies our discarded love.
Hats and scarves
Warming what once was ours.

Like a series on Netflix
You never quite finish.
The what-ifs and cliffhangers,
Unresolved, un-missed.

Love Me Hate Me

Kiss me
Cuss me
Lick me
Fuck me
Take me to
Ecstasy.

Love who you will

Who am I

To tell you

How to be

Happy.

Milano

For the
First time
In
Forever,
I don't want you.
How bittersweet.

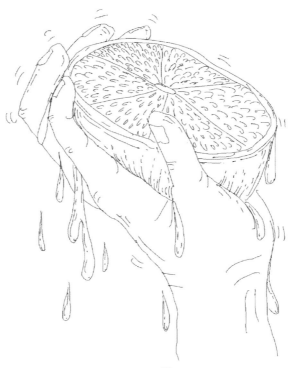

Mount Olympus

Mount Olympus
Where I live
Land of Gods
And ancient myths.

Mount Olympus
Where I sleep
Place where mortals
Seek to eat.

Mount Olympus
Here I am.
But where are you?
Where will we meet?

My Broken Pieces

I don't want my broken pieces to be fixed
Stuck back together
Or pushed, or pulled, or screwed back into place.

I don't want to forget the pain you caused me.
I don't want to forget how in every break, I learned there could be
New light glinting off my edges.

All of my broken pieces
Axed off me,
One by one.

Some, imperceptible.
The tiniest of grating, chipping
Gently filing as my edges disappear in stardust.

Then hammering, axe-ing
A bulldozer to the ground
Shaking my foundations and my core.

I was a beautiful piece of carbon graphite.
Deep in colour,
Pure in clarity.

My broken pieces falling off me
Losing parts of myself
Crying out to the world
The pressure unbearable,

As if crushing every inch of my soul,
Help!
Until –
I realised,
You made me into a diamond.

My Heart is a Palace

My heart is a Palace.
At times empty, forlorn.
I hear the echo of my own footsteps.
I am alone.

Sometimes people knock at the door.
A thick, oak, arched door
Double height
Bolted from within.

Some knock hard, furious,
Battering at my gate.
Some knock, quieter, so soft they barely make a sound.
All are heard.

But few are welcome
Or welcomed.
For the entrance lies not at the door
But at the window, round the side.

Why don't I open the door?
It's not that I'm short of space,
My palace has enough rooms to house
And replenish even the most weary of souls.

But I've been ravaged one too many times.
The door stays shut and,
Perhaps, now the window too.
Window of opportunity - or so they call it.

Dust gathers on the chandelier,
The ballroom is out of use.
I miss the dancing and the music,
My palace is fit for a recluse.

My last visitor came in disguise
In the middle of the night.
I thought he was here to stay
But he recently took flight.

I don't even know how he got in?
But he did.
Barrelled oak doors are no match
For a Persistent Prince (or is he a pauper?).

The palace came alive.
The birds sang, fruit grew,
The garden flowered.
We had balls and banquets,

We feasted, on Love alone.
He made my palace his Home.
My home. Our home.
It was his doing alone.

He painted the walls crimson red
With golden drapes.
The finest vases adorned
The marble mantelpieces.

Fresh flowers at every turn,
A place so full of life and joy
I couldn't believe it was my own.
I came alive.

But change came like a hurricane,
The Prince now Perpetrator
In a self-destructive rage
Destroys his belongings, undoes what was his doing.

Wreaking havoc at every turn,
An unstoppable force
Destroying everything.
He smashed the vases,

Left the flowers to wilt,
Pulled down the curtains,
Lost the jewellery,
Stained the crimson red walls.

The palace was broken,
Defenceless,
A sea of people still banging at its doors -
But can't they see? There's nothing left inside.

Windows are shattered,
Shards of glass on the floor
Cutting my feet every time I try to move forwards.
My heart is broken.

New Life

Even as I'm sat here, writing this poetry,
I wonder "why?"

Why do I continue to give myself to you,
To write these poems, because of you?

It's not like you didn't have the opportunity
To love me, to hold me; to be loved, by me.

I read 14:58 to Solinne, she liked it
But said that you weren't deserving of it.

"I like the poem but I don't like what he did to you.
He doesn't deserve the poem. He doesn't deserve you."

But the Poetry isn't for you.
It is for me.

It is about feeding my soul and freeing my anxiety,
Finding peace amidst the chaos,

Beauty amongst the rubble,
New beginnings in endings.

It is about finding life in death.

NWTKE

I wake up and I realise I'm alone.
The pain hits me all over again,
Like a wave crashing against a rock.

I saw you in my dream again last night.
My brain is treacherous like that.
Makes me happy asleep only to be devastated once more.

Sometimes I cry in the shower
With "the lonely hour" playing.
I don't know what to do with myself,
Without you.

I found my grey sweater this morning,
The one that's soft like a cloud.
It reminded me of you, of lying next to you.
Turns out it had traces of you, too.

I heard Dido's White Flag
And the tears came rushing
Crushing my soul
In a waterfall of emotion.

I'm in love.
I was. I am.
I'm not good with endings, or loss.
I never have been.

I see reminders of you everywhere.
My lips still burn at the thought of your touch.
Is this madness or simply despair?
My brain is treacherous & the feeling too much.

I can't bear the thought of losing you.
The irony is the thought of losing you was worse than the reality.
It's not just pain I feel now,
So much as that I've lost a part of me.

I still hold out hope that there's more,
More stories to write and dreams to share,
That you'll call me up and tell me you want to be there.
With me. Together.
You'd be the Drake to my Rihanna,
But our fairytale wouldn't end.

Together we'd travel the world both near and far,
Different countries, different dreams,
Playing songs on your guitar
And maybe we'd record them as I'd sing along
With my made up lyrics to your favourite song.

I want what we had, can't you see?
I can't understand why you don't want me.

I want to be cooking in the kitchen
Whilst you creep up behind me,
Wrap your arms around my waist,
Kiss my neck, hold me tight, love me deeply,
Whisper in my ear that I'm the perfect woman,
Or am I crazy, because there must be something wrong with me, surely?
How is it that someone like me loves a panda like you?
No, I'm not crazy, I'm just crazy for you.
Fuck clichés but fuck me it's true.

It still astounds me that it astounded you.
I wish you could see yourself through my eyes.

And from the kitchen to the living room to the bedroom,
We had our own universe in each other's eyes; easily satisfied.
When you held me, the whole world stopped.
And I felt whole.
When you kissed me my heartbeat raced and I couldn't help but smile.
I often kissed you smiling. I never knew that "smiling kisses" were a thing.
That is how much joy, pure unadulterated, unfiltered, untainted joy I felt.
SO MUCH: that I couldn't even contain it between my two lips.

As I climbed the stairs to your flat, 2 at a time out of anticipation and excitement, my
stomach filled with butterflies.
When you kissed my neck, held my hand, stroked my hair,
Hugged me tight with arms and legs intertwined like a deep rooted tree,
Celebrated my accomplishments, made fun of me also,
When you brought me down to earth.
When you sat with me and just listened.
When you could just look into my eyes and know what was going on.
I've never been an open book but you read me like I was your only language.

I opened up to you. I gave my heart to you.

The truth is: I chose you.

I will never be the same again.

Ode to Egypt

The wheels come out of the plane

I see a maze of lights below

Touch down.

I am home.

I breathe in your smell

Which I cannot describe

But it is distinctively yours.

I smile.

It is funny how you have grown

To be my place of comfort

My place of rest

My home

When you were once

So foreign to me.

You still fill me

With curiosity.

Living is not always

An easy ride

But coming home

Makes the ride worthwhile.

Masr, I love you.

Ode to My Body

My body showed me the world
My body swam in free water lakes
My body jumped into the sea and ran on the sand
My body skied down mountains
My body took me to see stars and suns and moons.
My body loved you.

My body is strong
My body is fierce
My body is loving
My body is powerful
My body is fearless
My body is mine.

Ode to Pants

Pants truly are the best
Knickers, bloomers,
And the rest!

Thongs, cheekinis
Bikinis too
Underwear, how I love you.

Pants, you make my world go round
Keep me soft, safe and sound
Pants you are glorious
Heavenly and victorious

Pants how I love you so
Pants, please! Never go
Always stay and hug my buttocks
Without you I'd be truly flummoxed.

'On This Day'

You are there for them,

You listen to them,

You help them,

You love them,

- and then?

You lose them.

Oslo

Bouncing up and down

In bountiful glee

I can't believe

I have a friend like You

Who loves me for me.

Pedestal

I'm told I'm on a pedestal
And yet how can I be?
When you are no longer here,
No longer next to me.

I'm told I'm on a pedestal
That to love me is a gift.
Why then when I'm without you,
Do I feel bereft?

I'm told I'm on a pedestal
That I should not give myself too soon.
Not open my heart to the bandits
Under a bright full moon.

I'm told I'm on a pedestal
But where does that leave me?
Does it mean I'm unreachable
Or a challenge for your team?

I'm told I'm on a pedestal
And maybe it's no bad thing after all.
For if I'm on a pedestal
You can catch me when I fall.

Perspective

I feel betrayed when I see my friends
Laughing with you.
I feel jealous as I see them
Speaking to you.
Dancing with you
Drinking with you
Enjoying pieces of you
That no longer belong to me.

Powerless

I can do so many things

Of that I am sure.

I can dance, I can ski, I can sing

I can swim to any shore.

I am smart, I am strong, I am fierce.

I am fun, I am light, I am Queen.

I am powerful and fearless

I live life like it's a dream.

But the one thing

I cannot do

Is to force love

Out of you.

Priorities

I wrote you
A poem
Which you never
Even read.

What does that say about you?
What does that say about me.

Promise me no promises

I don't want false fucking promises
I don't want to be filled with despair
When it inevitably ends.

*

Don't promise me the moon;
Give me the sun.

Don't sweet talk me at night;
Show me love in the day.

There is no truth amongst the shadows;
Only doubts and inconsistencies.

Love me in the light;
Where everyone can see.

Don't let our boat capsize
At first sight of a wave;

All hands on deck,
Keep us even-keeled.

Let the waves wash over us;
The storm will pass.

Batten down the hatches;
Take refuge with me.

When the sun comes out again
We will sail three sheets to the wind;

High on life,
Love will fill our sails and our souls;

By the time we reach land
We will know the ropes.

*

Promise me nothing
And only then
Will I know it's real.

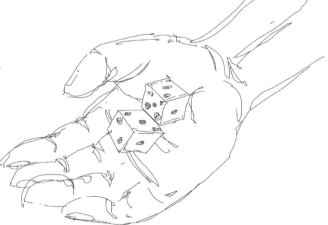

Puppets

I feel sorry for you
Truly I do
To lose a love so great.

When I see you
All over her social media
I know you are just trying to forget.

As if to convince yourself
That in liking her
You are un-liking me.

Why then don't you show her to the world?
Why is it only in places solely she can see?

If you are truly that happy
Then show the world!
Don't hide behind fake promises
And Instagram kisses.

What a joke.

Do you even know yourself?
Are you that oblivious?

Open your eyes
Smell the coffee
You're unhappy!

Stop trying to numb the pain
Accept that you're the one to blame.

Purpose

I read the 40 Rules of Love
And in it I found you.

I realised your purpose was to
Make a Poet out of me.

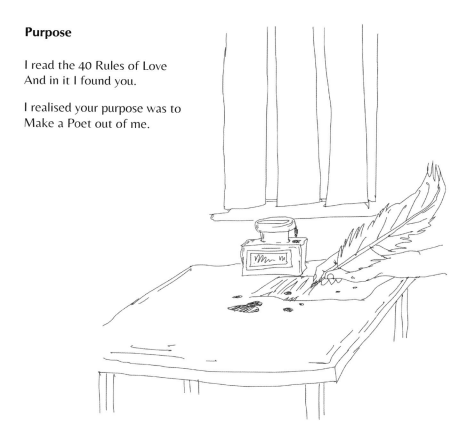

Regret (short-lived)

I was so insane to leave you.
What the fuck was I thinking?

Repeat views

You say that it's over
You say you don't care,
Then why do your visits
Reek of despair?

Every day I see you
Looking at my page,
I wish it wasn't so
But it fills me with rage.

The devastation you have caused
Was enough the first time.
Be gone. Be free.
Move on without me.

Rhythm

The music is pounding
Sea air on our skin
Tequila on our lips
Stolen glances, once, twice
Fingers which tentatively collide
The rhythm filling our bodies
A hedonistic Saturday
Just one drink, just one glass
Just one shot, just one past
Grab my hand in the crowd
Dance with me, now
The promise of what is yet to come
Amidst the bodies
Moving
Shaking
Jumping
Swaying
We are strangers
Lost in the crowd.
Hi Grade on your mind
A smile on my lips
Take me now
Kiss me goodbye
By the secret garden steps.

SILENCIO

When did silence get so painful

Awkward, stuttering, strange, shameful

Once so close but now so far

What happened to the cookie jar

With all our hopes and dreams inside?

Now on the floor, we died beside.

Self-care

Nourish your aura.
Nourish your soul.

Your beauty and light
Shine bright.
Let it radiate through you.

No matter whether you are
Heavier, Lighter
Fatter, Thinner
With hair that's longer or shorter
Skin that's clear or breaking out.

Those things
Do not define you.
Your aura does.

Nourish your aura.
Nourish your soul.

Self-loathing

When did I get so arrogant
To think I could cheat
Myself?

When did I become so foolish
To think I could fool around
Without falling apart?

When did it become OK
To sell myself short
For a fling?

For someone who clearly said
They weren't looking for anything?

Was it when, the first night, you pulled me
In for a kiss under the shooting stars?
Was it when, on your balcony,
You slipped two fingers inside me
Or was it when you had me pushed against a wall,
Groaning, asking for more,
As you kissed my ears, my nose, my lips
Bringing my senses alive
My hips thrusting forward
Ready to meet you,
Inviting you in.
Your mouth travelling south
My stomach tight from the anticipation.
My eyes not knowing where to look,
Closed tight, praying that this was real.

Was it when we started holding hands,
My thumb drawing circles, your fingers squeezing mine,
Was it when we were guilty teenagers,
Stealing kisses behind closed doors and in the sea,
As you carried me over waves and I hoped you would hold me
forever.
"You're so nice. Please don't leave" you said to me,
"Then stay. Don't let me go" my heart cried back,
But my mouth didn't speak a word.
I've been here before you see,
And what I really need is consistency.
How to know if you truly want me?

Was it when, on your rooftop,
You kissed me and time stopped
As you wrapped your arms around me.
Was it as you rocked me in your hammock, and held me.
Was it when you told me flights would be cheap for me to visit -
and I thought maybe you would want something after all?

Was it each time we lay there,
Asleep in each other's arms.
Was it as you bit me once, twice
"enough biting or I'll eat you up entirely".
Was it when you put your arms around me,
For everyone to see?

Is that when it happened?
Was I betrayed by the false sense of security
That comes from publicity?

Or maybe it was real. And maybe it was true.
But I sold myself short.
And that's something I should never have done.
For you.

Selfishness

You wanted me
Pursued me
Even though you knew
You couldn't complete me.

Made me fall for you
But it was all a lie.
Left me by surprise
A lifetime to cry.

If I asked you
Why you did it.
I'm sure that
You would say

"How could I not try it?
Your light
Brightened up
My day"

You took a part of me
To keep for yourself
Left me here wounded
And bleeding out.

Not even a plaster
To cover the pain
Took what you needed
And skipped out on the game.

Hear me now though,
Traitor.
I will pine for you
No more.

Keep your selfishness.
Take it back.
I don't need it.
I don't need you.

I will find
Someone
Who can love me
For me.

The Bay

My heart didn't break

Because

I left you.

I left

Because

You broke my heart.

The Bay 2

You told me that you loved me
You said you'd never leave
You said we had to make it through
That all would work with ease.

You told me you supported me
That you were proud of what I did
But as soon as you went and travelled abroad
You forgot me. Just a blip.

Sisters

Every person who has had an impact on me this year
Has had a sister.
Not just a sister,
A Sister.
A sister they cared for
A sister they loved
A sister they nurtured
A sister they lost.
And maybe all of these people
Were sent to cross my path
To teach me love is eternal,
True love does last.
And maybe the common
Denominator of all
Was my sister, Anouchka
And not me at all.

Soft Tissue Injury

EMOTIONAL

WHIPLASH.

Solinne

Solinne
I wish you could
See yourself
The way the world sees you.
A warrior.
A goddess.
Your strength radiates out of you
Your light chases away the darkness
A beauty so bright
It could power a universe.
Yes, he has left you.
But you have not left yourself.
A temple is not defined by its worshippers,
A temple houses God within.
God has not left you.
Some days the pain will weigh heavy
It will numb your soul
And cloud your eyes
And you will wonder if you will ever see again.
Until the fog lifts
And you will glimpse
A whole world left to discover.
Bright and colourful
The contrast will be blinding.
A world that is ready for you.
A world for you to love.
A world of love.

Special Needs

When people look at you
I wonder what they see?
Do they see a different nose
A different face
Do they see your hearing aids
Your feeding tube
Your tracheostomy scar
Do they see that you can't speak
The same way that they do
Do they feel pity
Or maybe they feel shame
For staring at someone who isn't to blame.

Stephanie's Table

I sat at Stephanie's table
This time one year ago
I told her that I loved you
I told her it was so.

I sit at Stephanie's table
One year on from then
I tell her that I'm done with love,
I cannot deal with men.

How long will I sit here?
How old will I be?
When will I sit at Stephanie's table
With the one meant for me?

Subconscious

I wonder what world is within you,
I wonder of what you dream?
Do I make you cry with joy
Or do I make you scream?
When you close your eyes at night
Who is it that you see?
Am I part of your desires
Or do they never feature me?
What is it that you're hiding
Somewhere deep within?
In this other world you call your mind
Only you can win.
Sometimes I think that I know you
Sometimes I think that you care
Until you close your eyes and I wonder
If you're even there.

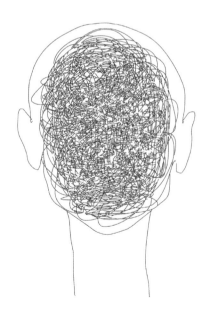

Summer

The sun was glinting
On the waves,
Blinding sparkles
Of summer,
Of hope.
Your head bobbing
In and out of sight,
I squinted to see you better.
You told me that
When you think of water
That's where magic happens.
I swam towards you
You put your arms around me
Carried me over a wave.
Make magic with me.

Summer nights

As the summer night sleeps
And white orchids look over me
The rustle and the breeze
Are the only thing I see.

I think the moon may be here
But I cannot say for sure
Her glow cast down upon us
Like a loving benefactor.

Summer nights – 2

Where will I find safety
When will I find home
Or am I simply destined
To live my life alone?

You sit there and tell me
You're not looking for anyone.
What then am I doing here
I should get up and run!

But my body will not move this time
It wants to find a home.
I sigh and fall asleep in your arms
Hoping one day I will learn.

Summer nights – 3

I look at you
As you watch the curtains billow:
Strips of white waving in the wind.

"I could sit here forever"
But it's not me you say it to.
The Beauty you seek lies elsewhere.

Summer nights – 4

I want to write you a poem
But of what, I'm not too sure.
Do you like me as much today
As you did before?

I still don't know our story
Or what it's to become
Is it one of love and hope
Or one from which I should run?

I could write about all the beautiful things
I felt and you said to me.
But were they just as real to you
As they were to me?

Because before I write you a poem
And let my heart sing in song.
I have to have felt the feelings
And known it wasn't wrong.

Tattoo

"Non omnis moriar"

I shall not wholly die

Your shoulder tells me.

Without you

I shall not wholly live

My heart tells me.

Tattoo 2

I wonder what you're up to now
Did you get your new tattoo?
The one of the astronaut
Looking up at you.

I wonder what you're up to now
How are your hopes and dreams?
Are they filled with life and joy,
Bursting at the seams?

I wonder what you're up to now
Do you ever think of me?
Even though all is said and done,
It's still a mystery.

The Mask

Do not be scared when I am sad.
Do not shy away if I cry.
It's when I smile you should be scared.
For my smile hides a thousand lies.

The Elephant in the room

You pull your penis out
"I've shown you a good time,
Now it's up to you to show me a good time."
I had asked you to take me home.
You led the way not to your car
But to your bedroom.
I hadn't realised
Kissing someone
Was consent for sex.
And as you stood there
Manhood hanging out
Not even erect
I couldn't help thinking it looked
Like an elephant.
Not because it was big,
But because it was so grey.
Grey! And wrinkly.
How is it that a 20-something
Had a trunk so aged?
It was practically staring me in the face,
I half expected it to trumpet.
What a circus.
The answer - as it had been 20 minutes earlier
Was no. Still no.
"Can I at least rub it against you?"
Are you fucking kidding me?
Although A+ for asking.

Christin.
  Fast forward 2 months
    You ask me out for drinks
      I go along, part naivety,
        Part respect for your parents.
        That was when you ask me
        To have an affair.
          Or rather, casual sex.
          You have a long term girlfriend
          You live together
          She's French too
          But you're just so sick of
          Fucking the same body
          And you need to fuck someone else
          Who you know will keep your secret.
          Christ.
        The answer - as it had been 2 months
        earlier
       Was no. Still no.
      Leave aside the obvious -
      What could there possibly be in it for me?!
    "Well for me, it's a night of casual sex"
    Yes, I got that bit.
  "For you? Oh, well.
I hadn't really thought about that."
  When people ask me why I'm single,
I tell them about
The Elephant in the room.

The Maybe-One

How do you know that someone's
The One?
Do you wait for it to become undone?
Is that a sign it was true love
When your heart is broken and floods with tears?

Or is The One simple, tranquil,
A welcome guest
A safe place, a Home
Somewhere to rest
Your tired body and weary heart.

Is The One he who carries you
Up flights of stairs
To parties perhaps
Or to transcendence
Who unites your bodies and souls.

Does The One fulfil you
And your wildest dreams
Is he your best friend, your confidante
Your fantasist
And fantasy.

Is The One attractive
Does he conform
Does he share your values and ideals
Does he excite you, challenge you
Take you beyond your comfort zone.

Does The One make you cry?
Does true love hurt?
Is true love easy? Painful?
Does true love make you laugh?
Is true love to be equated with The One?

Or is The One within you
Is he defined by your thoughts
By your emotions, your compromises
By the small moments only you can see,
Only you can feel.

Can you know someone is The One,
Can it be True Love
And yet they not feel the same?
Can The One be unrequited love?
How to know if their feelings are real?

Is The One he who stays
Amongst bleary weeks and gloomy days
And sits by the fire
Fuelled by desire
For You.

What is the language of Love?
What is The One
Is it real?
I don't know.
Do you?

The Problem with Betrayal

The problem with betrayal
Is it makes me question everything.
Your motives, your behaviour,
Even the good times.
Like when you told me,
Asked me even,
What was a girl like me doing on Bumble?
That I was worth so much more than a dating app could offer.
That I was incredible.
That I didn't need to be on there.
Did you mean what you said?
Or did you just not want me to find you still on there?
Did you want to keep me all to yourself,
Whilst you would never truly belong to me?

Therapy

I spent a year getting to know myself

And I liked who I met.

Tomb Raider

The more I fight
The memories
The more
They flood me.

Like bullets, searing through me.

An image of your face,
A kick in the teeth.
I see your place so clearly that it scares me.
I feel you climb into bed next to me
As another bullet whizzes past me.
You kiss me goodnight
Pull me tight
Just as I'm ambushed by my reverie.
I wish I could say I'm a fighter
But right now I resemble
A warrior lost in the jungle.
Battered and bruised,
I push the leaves away
But it's no use
They just hit back.
Covered now in soil, in blood
When will it stop?
Please. Stop.
I see your smile. I crave your kiss. I feel your touch.
A slap. A punch. A kick.
Will I make it out of the jungle alive?
I don't know if this time I'll survive.

v2

What is it that you see in her?
Tell me. What do you see?
Can't you see she's just a Beta
Downgraded version of me?

Why would you choose Prosecco
When you could have Mumm?
Prosecco, yes, affordable
But drunk by everyone.

What is it that you see in her?
Tell me. What do you see?
She isn't even beautiful
And surely can't love you like me.

Views

I imagine you both sitting on your sofa.

Furtively looking at your phones.

Not knowing
That each of you
Is reading
Me.

Oh, the irony!

One, who loved me. Who lost me.
One, who despises me. Having been loved by him before her.
Bitterness, mixed with curiosity.

The potency of
Emotion
Distilled
Into each
Inhale.
Exhale.

Breathe.

I'm still here.

Visceral

I feel

Sick

To my

Stomach

When I

See You

With

Her.

What if...

What if my heart never heals?

Wildfire

The devastation you have caused
Spreading like a wildfire.
Unthinkable.
A ravine
Welded into someone's heart.
So deep it may never heal.
The ground so burnt,
So sparse
That even if it rains,
Even if someone tries
To quench the drought,
The land will reject the water
The soil too damaged by the hurt.

Wishful Thinking

Why did I mistake the dead end sign,
Accompanied by a glaring forbidden entry sign,
Standing proudly at the top of your road
For an invitation to enter?
As if I could singlehandedly
Rewrite the rules
You laid down
For yourself.

20:20 vision

I don't wear my lenses
As I walk down your street,
On my way back from boxing
It's only strangers I meet.

I may have come across you
But I really wouldn't know,
I smile as I walk on
But the smile is just for show.

Sometimes I look up at your window
And wonder if you're there,
But I walk on past and know full well
You're no longer mine to share.

But even if I saw you
Somewhere in the street,
You wouldn't see me anyway:
For our souls are yet to meet.

14:58

And as the sadness seeps through me
And the days go by
The pain washes over
The sting of goodbye.

You left me here standing
My back to a wall
Almost feels like We
Never happened at all.

And though the tears dry
As I lay in my bed
I can't help but wonder
If you meant what you said?

Were we real? Was it true?
You said you would stay.
Did you feel the same too
Or did you fill with dismay

And run at the sight
Of seeing me here
Open, vulnerable, Christ!
Honest, sincere.

Is this what happens
When I open my heart?
Abandoned, betrayed
Left alone in the dark.

And for now, though you're gone
I think of you still.
There's no moving on
Just time standing still.

Thank You

I suppose I should say Thank You
For breaking my heart
You helped create and inspire
All of this art.

You took me to places
I never had been
You made me your Queen
I made you my King.

If I think of you now
It fills me with love
You showed me places
I couldn't dream of.

You sparked a fire in me
That brought me to life;
Healed the pain of the past
Calmed internal strife.

You were fulfilling, replenishing
For my body and soul.
Gave me hope for the future,
Nurtured me whole.

You made me feel things
I couldn't even imagine,
You showed me love
In the ultimate fashion.

You brought out the best in me.
For that I am thankful.

Epilogue

Breakup survival tips from me to myself and all of you:

1. Cry. A lot. Let it out.

2. Exercise. Sweat it all out. A lot.

3. Routine. Be it in the form of weekly therapy or weekly spinning. It helps to have something to look forward to. If you do it on Wednesdays: it's a nice way to break up the week and means you only have to take everything two days at a time.

4. Rupi Kaur poetry books. Read them. Cry. Feel less alone.

5. FRIENDS. Coffees, brunches, movie nights. Whatever it is: FRIENDS. NB only friends who actually make you feel good about yourself. No time or energy for anyone's negativity in times like these.

6. FOOD: DON'T EAT CRAP. It will make you feel worse in the long run. And no one wants to be me six months down the line with half a stone of grief hanging off your body.

7. Khalid's American Teen album. Perfect mix of indulging in sad emotions yet uplifting. He is a genius.

8. "All The Feels" playlist on Spotify. Also good for those days when you want music but can't handle The Spice Girls.

9. Don't feel embarrassed or ashamed about whatever it is you're feeling. It's human and normal.

10. Believe in yourself and know that you will emerge from this whole.

11. You are not alone. Don't withdraw. Reach out to people who make you feel loved.

12. You are worthy of love.

Love you all x

About the author

Emily is a poet, yoga teacher and barrister living in London.

Printed in Great Britain
by Amazon